STILL HERE

STILL HERE

ROWAN BLANCHARD

RAZORBILL®

An Imprint of Penguin Random House
Penguin.com

RAZORBILL & colophon is a registered trademark
of Penguin Random House LLC.

First published in the United States of America by Razorbill,
an imprint of Penguin Random House LLC, 2018

LIBRARY OF CONGRESS CATALOGING-IN-PUBLICATION DATA IS AVAILABLE

ISBN 9780448494661

Printed in Canada

1 3 5 7 9 10 8 6 4 2

Cover Design by Theresa Evangelista
Interior Design by Maria Fazio

Dear reader,

Here you are, welcome to *Still Here*.

This is, above all, a piece of a young heart. The confusion of being born, of being born too old, of looking too young. When you ask someone to believe you, and they do. Standing alone in the bathroom during a party, how did I get here, why am I here, do they notice me. This is raw rage, commonly referred to by adults regarding teens as Angst, but I see it as something deeper than that, something that cannot be contained in one word. I believe this rawness, this anger, this sadness, this wonder is possibly the time where our feelings are the most sincere. When our gazes are still somewhat informed by our own unknowingness, when we are intoxicated and addicted to how it feels to experience something for the first time.

This book, which I think of as more of an art project that has molded into this form, is a first of many things for me. It is October of 2017 when I write this. I have just passed my sixteenth birthday, which marks roughly the three-year anniversary of when I began molding this idea. I always had slightly older friends. I got to watch quintessential teen life happen to my friends, years before it would happen to me: anxiously hearing their stories of first kisses, watching them sneak off to go to parties, hearing how they were going to come out to their parents or not. The day they found that one Nirvana song that spoke to them that suddenly contained an entire universe. I got to watch them (from the backseat) roll down the window and blast their favorite song. I remember the first time I watched a friend stick their head out the window and I thought, One day that will happen to me, and that must be how it feels to know you are an infinite, small piece of the universe. A constant re-realization of yourself as a dot on the Earth; that will come as a comfort. How it feels like everyone is watching you, when really, no one is watching you. How it looks to not care. I got to watch all of it. I knew because adults had told me, "These years will be the worst of your life," and in a way, they have felt that way. There is so much feeling and everything is so intense, sometimes I wonder if I might die. I do not mean that in a cynical or depressed tone, but in more ways than one, growing up is a series of weird funerals — you are shedding so many old ways, an old body, what it meant to not have responsibilities, what it meant to maintain innocence, what it meant to not be looked at.

I assume I was attracted to, and least intimidated by, making something about this very specific time because growing up is such a void. There is so much space! So many uncolored, so many un-worded feelings! What would it mean if I explored that empty space? If I asked my friends, if I reached out to people I knew from the internet to explore that space? Maybe, and hopefully, I have made something that speaks to what it means to occupy new space, which is maybe another phrase for having to grow up and outward, to find the space that works for you or maybe, merely, the space you grow to fit.

It humbles me to think about how things have changed since the origin of this book you are holding. It scares me, somewhat, that this is in your hands now. But I want to trust you, and I want you to trust me that everything in here is exactly how it felt in the moment. I am too quick to diminish my own work as dramatic and embarrassing, but of course it is. I am the one who thought of giving you my own diary entries after all, so really it is my fault, but I am learning that a lot of this growing-up thing is mostly just accepting that a lot happens when the moment simply sweeps you up and life hits you all at once; when this happens at its best, the world becomes stunning.

I wonder what it means to grow up right now. On this date, October 26th, 2017, he is still the president of the United States, and I fear walking outside in an outfit that I feel hot in because just what if. I don't want my friends to lose their basic rights. Most of my memories of this past year are of protests, or being in cars with friends, crying with friends, stunned at the news, not knowing what advice to offer. My friends are young and just want to be themselves, they just want to survive, but people go on TV and tell us they hate people like us, and I catch us hoping that if we hold each other close enough, if we tell each other so desperately that we love each other, maybe the world will become small enough to hold us safely just for a moment.

There is a piece of hope that I do try to remind myself of as a comfort, because even if it doesn't cure me in that moment, it is still a fact: despite living underneath our different and/or shared isms or something like this administration, we are all still here, still here, still here. I know that. I have to know that. This work comes from various times in people's lives; some of these pieces I wrote at twelve or thirteen, of course dramatic and sad, but mostly just honest. We have been fighting. We have been thinking, writing, capturing, observing, sometimes hoping. The world is such a big place. Samera Paz's photo from the Freddie Gray protests in Baltimore, Arabelle Sicardi's urgent ballad about what it means to survive—these are our stories, our pledges, sometimes our cries out. This is truth. I hope this finds you when you need it, I hope it finds its way into your heart, that we listen to each other and, most magically, see ourselves in each other. This is a tiny, fragile microcosm of how it feels to grow up. I'm still figuring that part out.

Here is *Still Here*, in its imperfections and quiet profoundness. I am glad you found it.

With love,

ROWAN

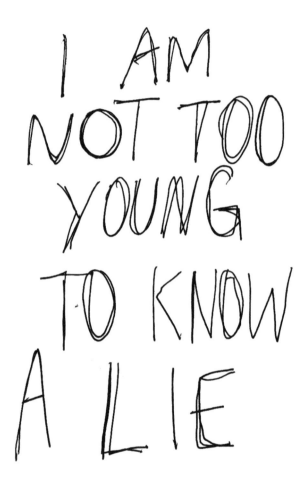

I AM
NOT TOO
YOUNG
TO KNOW
A LIE

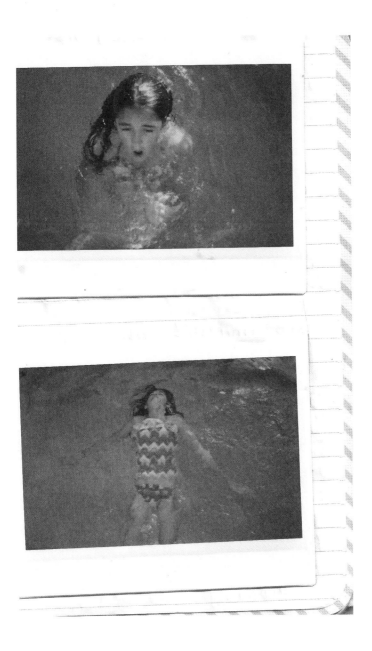

8/6/06

One day a new bunch of kittins was born. there names were kelly, anne, kally, toni, courthy and Bailey. they loved each other very much. but one day there mom died. the kittens got separated. they were sad.

At fashion week me and Skyler went to the village at 2:30 am and went to a "party" at two 30 year olds apartment named Jesse and Kiroh but no one else came except us and they gave us weird vibes and we lied to them about our entire lives and they were really drunk and Kiroh said something about AA and Jesse was doing blow on their kitchen counter and Kiroh was trying to use me as a photog for her modeling career and they put on music it was a bad Weeknd song so we made up an excuse and left

Any time I am in need
of a depressing
event to freshen up
my life, I always have
my birthday coming

But the takeaway point is I learned how good it is to be out of your comfort zone

TODAY my family and I drove home from champs for dinner and Age of Consent came on

(my birthday)

it was as if someone had spread
butter across all the fine points
of the stars because when he
looked up they started to slip

DORCAS
Cure

IM SORE FROM ALL THIS GROWING

I Hope one ... day all ... become a beautiful flower

I pretend there is
no time slipping
away from me
but that doesn't make
it hurt less it just
puts makeup on a
bruise

What to do with all this time

I am so scared of all this time

My room is a mess

I am so tired

all the time

I can't figure out why

Maybe its just the mind

Do you think if I stay up all night

time will go slower?

02.11. 6

I went inside the ocean by myself today. It was
really cold like the kind of cold that could be
used to torture someone. I like how cold it makes
me because one by one, each of your limbs stops
going against it. It feels nice to be inside of something
that isnt so easy to fall into. the water has to hold
its patience long enough for you to walk into it. I like
to walk slowly into the water. I also like to jump into
it. I like not knowing her. I was in there for an hour
looking straight ahead and her body is always
settling into itself and returning back to her. Its
like she tries to shed her own skin.

I dont understand her so i have to keep ripping
her open.

I like to rush into her like we're friends that
havent seen eachother in a while. I smile to her—
she knows something I dont.
I feel her presence but i want her to figure
out the linings of my body.
I want her to part my arms and legs and
find the exit of my skin. I want the water
to breathe inside of my throat. I want to
become her.

IM GIVING
YOU AWAY
TO THE
WHOLE WORLD

July 15 2000
2:35 am

26

AND SUDDENLY GRIEF
COMES BACK 7 MONTHS
LATER

WHERE DO YOU GO TO?
YOU'RE UNDER MY PILLOW,
IN MY COFFEE
IN A SENTENCE IN ANY BOOKS

WHY DO YOU HIDE WITH NO
WARNING?

I CAN FEEL MY FACE
STARED STILL WET

I CAN'T FEEL MY FACE
STILL WET

I
HAVE NEVER LIED ABOUT YOU
YOU'RE STINGING MY EYES
AND WAKING UP MY FAMILY.

27

I PROMISE TO BELIEVE YOU
IF YOU TELL ME YOU
ARE HURTING

To feel pain is not living to the fullest
brush it aside, breathe in
forget it for a moment
don't give them the satisfaction
    of tears
give them the satisfaction
    of their loss

I tell all my friends
if you're going to cry, cry
    everything out right now
DONE?

brush away the tears still lingering
    on your cheeks
Inhale, and sigh
and never shed another tear again

Happiness is close at hand
so let me hold yours and guide you there
I promise, I will never give up on you
Scream at me, push me, throw me aside
I'll stand up again just to stand by you
Because what I see in you is potential
And potential is a gift too great to let slide
        UNOTICED

Nov 24/09

i found a butterfly wing in the grass yesterday and there were specks of silver on it that rubbed off on my fingers that made the spiral tracks on my finger tips sparkle. i wrapped it up to save for later but i decided to put it back in the grass because i didn't want it to break. i love quiet.

there are so many things i could do with my life

a little book to write my tears into ☺

i am laying at the beach in leo carillo and my hair feels so hot like in the summertime but the water is much colder in february than in june july or august.

"mechanical reproduction in the age of technology"

what does it mean for me to be the image / the portrait / the character of the naked woman over and over again?

strangers think they really know me

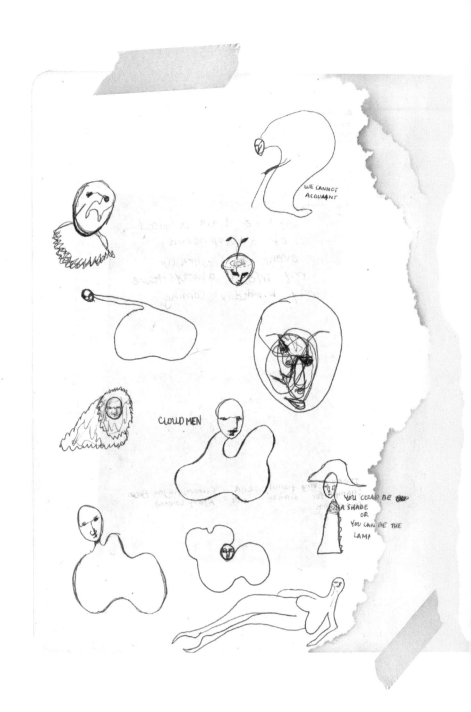

WE CANNOT
ACQUAINT

CLOUD MEN

YOU COULD BE
A SHADE
OR
YOU CAN BE THE
LAMP

ONE DAY I WILL
RECGIONIZE ALL THE WAYS
THAT YOU'VE HURT ME
BUT UNTIL
THEN
IT ONLY HURTS TO PRETEND.
IT HAPPENED TO ME. I THOUGHT
I KNEW TO SPEAK UP AND
USE MY VOICE BUT
I DIDN'T. FIND IT IN THAT
MOMENT I WAS JUST
REALLY CONFUSED
AND I DON'T KNOW WHAT
I WANTED OTHER
THAN MAYBE SOMEONE
TO DRIVE ME FAR FAR
INTO THE MIDDLE OF
THE NIGHT WHICH IS
WHERE I ENDED UP
ANYWAY

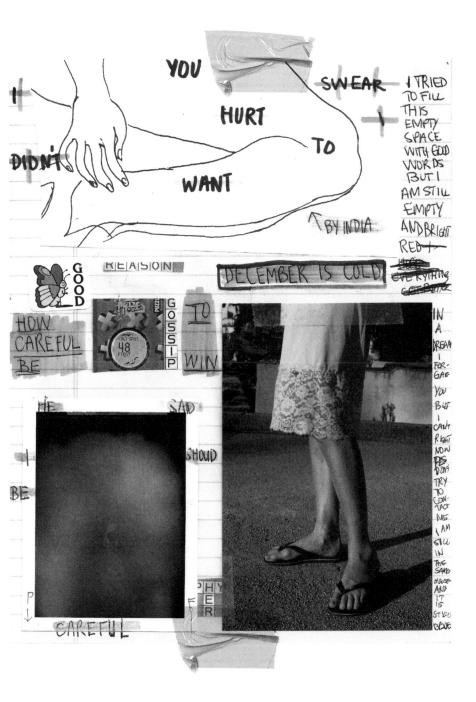

YOU HURT TO WANT SWEAR
I DIDN'T

I TRIED TO FILL THIS EMPTY SPACE WITH GOOD WORDS BUT I AM STILL EMPTY AND BRIGHT RED

↑ BY INDIA

GOOD REASON DECEMBER IS COLD

HOW CAREFUL BE
GOSSIP TO WIN
I BE
HE SAID SHOULD
CAREFUL

IN A DREAM I FORGAVE YOU BUT I CAN'T RIGHT NOW PLS DON'T TRY TO CONTACT ME I AM STILL IN THE SAME HOUSE AND IT IS STILL BLUE

39

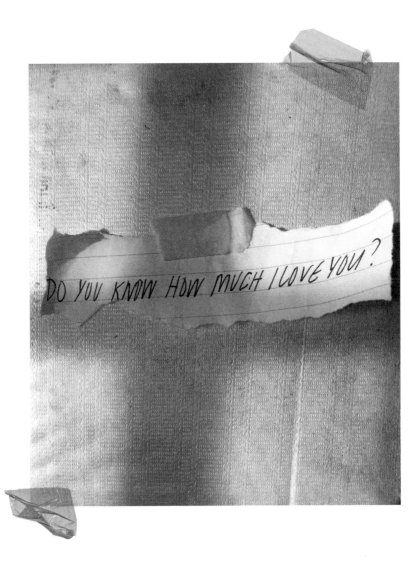

EVERYONE IS
GETTING SO BIG
:(

I WRITE THIS FROM BOOKSOUP ON
SUNSET ON THE TOP STAIR WITH
A BRAND NEW PEN.

THE WORLD IS SO BIG ~~I SEE~~
THAT I FEEL MYSELF TENSING AT
HAVING TO SEE IT CHANGE.

AS OF LATELY I HAVE BEEN
SO CONSUMED BY THE BLEAKNESS
OF MY AGE. IAM TOO OLD FOR
MYSELF AND TOO YOUNG FOR
OTHERS. MY GROWING PAINS TAKE
THE FORM OF FOGGY CAR
WINDOWS AND THE SIMPLICITY AND
MULTITUDES CONTAINED IN THE
WORDS "HOW DOES IT FEEL".

IT HAS FELT VERY COLD. I AM
FLOATING OVER MYSELF HALF
THE TIME, MY BODY IS MOVING
YET I AM COMPLETELY MOTIONLESS.
I GET ANXIETY CROSSING STREETS
BECAUSE THERE ARE SO MANY
CARS AND SO MANY LIVES THAT

ARE INCOMPLETE. ~~BUT VERY~~
~~TROUBLED KNOWING EVERYONE~~

I AM NOT AS SMALL AS
I USED TO BE. THIS IS MADE
AWARE TO ME BY HOW I HAVE
TO MOVE MY LEGS EVERY TIME
SOMEONE MOVES DOWN THE
STAIRS. ~~THEY~~
THE LYRICS "I DRANK TOO
MUCH LAST NIGHT" ARE
LOOPING OVER THE SPEAKERS.
FOR THE FIRST TIME,
I KNOW WHAT THEY MEAN.

WHAT PEOPLE DON'T
UNDERSTAND IS THAT THEY
SEE GHOSTS EVERY DAY.
I SEE HUNDREDS OF THEM
RIGHT NOW, LINING THE WALLS,
LEANING ON EACH OTHER. I
FEEL LIKE A GHOST NOW.
A GHOST IN MY OWN BODY.
MY BODY OUTPITTING THE
SOUL INSIDE.

I SEE GHOSTS OF MYSELF
EVERYWHERE. NOW THERE IS
A LOT OF TIREDNESS AND TOO
MUCH THINKING AND TOO LITTLE
TIME. THE OLD GHOSTS ARE
SPREAD OUT AROUND MY
PARENTS AND SOMETIMES SHOW
THEMSELVES. TRYING TO COEXIST
WITH THEM IS HARD AND ~~EX~~
EXHAUSTING BUT MY WORST

FEAR WOULD BE TO
ABANDON THEM. I FEEL
MYSELF SLOWLY DRIFTING
AWAY EVERY DAY WHICH
IS WHY I DON'T STAY IN
ONE PLACE FOR TOO LONG
AS MUCH AS I WOULD LIKE TO.
I HAVE TO KEEP UP WITH
THEM. YOU ARE LYING
IF YOU SAY YOU DON'T
BELIEVE IN GHOSTS.

43

IT IS SCARING ME THAT THERE
ARE SO MANY THINGS I
USED TO BELIEVE WITH
ALL OF MY HEART AND ALL
OF MY SOUL, ~~THE~~

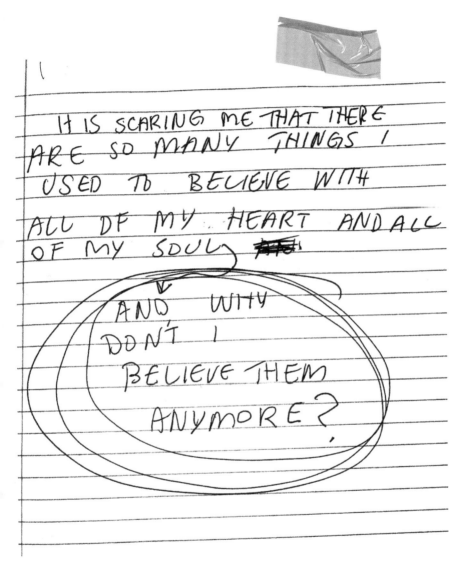

AND WHY
DON'T I
BELIEVE THEM
ANYMORE?

I was SCARED to go to the protest, no actually - hesitant or just unsure! I always want to make sure I don't show up and it's all white people - we've heard enough of their voices - we've been dominated far too long by their ideas, their tragedies, their obsessions, their shame, their greed

I have literally been asked by white people: "Why do you wish to destroy us?"
But no matter how many times POC, indigenous folks, black folks

Latinx folks, API folks, LGBTQ+
folks ask the same question
about literal genocide, literal
massacres, literal imprisonment,
literal detention, literal destruction

we are met with ... nothing.
WE DESERVE TO SURVIVE too ♡♡♂♡

Standing at JFK Terminal 4, I
couldn't say "LET THEM IN!"
because twenty-nine years ago, I
was "let" in. Or, I clawed my
way in ... or someone, many someones
clawed their way in so that
I and so many others could get
through!

Who are my true foremothers? The
ones who smashed the wall
I slipped through? I wish to
thank them ♡♡♡♡♡♡♡♡♡♡♡♡♡

We brought pizza to the protest but
I couldn't get any of the POC protesters
to accept a slice... only the white
kids accepted!

I don't want to see only whats wrong but I don't want to be part of some white person's guilt trip! I don't want to be used in their attempts to absolve themselves of complicity or responsibility.

NOW WE LIVE

IN A WORLD

WITH NO EASY ANSWERS

NO MORE CONQUESTS

NO MORE FIGHTING
ONLY FOR YRSELF!
PIPING UP WHEN YOU & YR
FAM R THREATENED
BUT SILENT AGAIN WHEN

IT'S SOMEONE ELSE!

Let this world live! Let this world survive

I AM
TRYING SO
HARD TO
SURVIVE BUT
DAMN YOU MOTHERFUCKERS
MAKE IT SO HARD!
I AM MAD AND
I AM CRYING BECAUSE
YOU WILL NEVER KNOW!
~~YOU WILL NEVER~~
~~KNOW~~

YOU WILL NEVER KNOW

WHAT I SEE,
SHOULD INFORM.

WHO CAN KNOW THE HEART
OF YOUTH
BUT YOUTH ITSELF?

she's full of rage

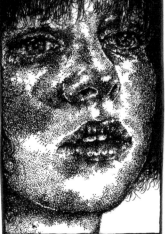

HERE COMES A FEELING YOU THOUGHT
YOU'D FORGOTTEN.
I DON'T WANT TO FEEL YOUR PAIN!!

I TOOK A PENCIL AND PUT A HOLE IN THE SKY.

I'M HUNGRY SHE SAID.
SO THEY FED HER
FAIRYTALES, MYTHS, CLASSICS, AND SONGS
IT WOULDN'T BE LONG UNTIL HANDS MOVED ACROSS
THE DIAL
HER PACE WAS DIFFERENT THOUGH
HIDDEN BEHIND THE FACE OF THE CLOCK
SHE WAS RUNNING ON THE BORDERS OF BORROWED TIME
SHE'D SEEN DEATH FROM THE MOMENT SHE STOOD
IN FRONT OF THE PAINTING OF
JESUS NAILED TO THE CROSS
IT WAS HIDING UNDER THE HEAVY BLACK SKIRTS
OF NUNS THAT GAVE HER SOLACE
SHE THOUGHT SHE'D LIVE ONLY TO THE AGE OF 33,
SO SHE RAN, HER GOOFY SMILE
AND LOVE WAS ALL SHE COULD GIVE
I HOPE I NEVER MAKE A HOME OUT OF SOMETHING
THAT MAKES ME WEAK.

51

BOYS NEED BACKBONES

AND WHY DON'T I BELIEVE THEM ANYMORE?

riding in cars with white boys

I once listened to a white boy talk about how Barack Obama isn't a black man to him, how he doesn't see color. I had a lot in common with this white boy. We both liked the Minneapolis-based band Cloud Cult and had strong opinions. He was a very good hug-giver and one time he rubbed my back, after our professor cut my caffeinated 20-minute presentation short.

I met a white girl from a town called Virginia around the same time I met the aforementioned white boy. When she was new to the city, she said the n-word around me and a mutual friend. She didn't really get why my friend (a white gay male) and I were offended and hurt but promised not to say the word again, which was a clear indication that she cared, even though she didn't understand. A couple months later, we found ourselves parked outside of Cub Foods with two of her friends from her Virginia. I had hung out with them before, at a party. They did that annoying thing a lot of white guys do: they made it clear they voted for Obama. I did that annoying thing I do: pretend I'm the DJ and make everyone listen to Soul Coughing. But shared politics and music be damned because white boys will be white boys. One of them said nigger and then before I knew it the other one said nigger. I got out the car and so did my friend and we walked twenty miles back to her truck parked across the city in the heat.

There's no litmus for being my friend. Just try not to hurt me and apologize if you do hurt me. I think that's all one can ask for. Colorblind white boy was a good friend to me in the brief time that I knew him and my friend from the hick town has been a good friend to me since the day we met. Good friends don't have to possess a knowledge of highfalutin critical theory or listen to the same music as you or share your preference for presidential candidates. Good friends just have to be there for the ride and know when to get out the car.

LETS MAKE
EVERYTHING ELSE
DISSAPEAR
TOGETHER

IM SO TIRED AND
SO STRESSED OUT AND
I WANT SOMEONE
WITH ME
WHO IS PERFECT
LIKE YOU
SO PLEASE
LET ME NOT REMEMBER
HOW IT FEELS
TO HAVE A
NAME

ALL THE MOMENTS ARE HERE!
ALL THE NIGHTS ARE HERE!
ITS ALL ABOUT THE NIGHTS NOW, BABY!

HOW LATE WILL YOU GO?
WHERE WILL YOU CRASH?
DO YOU WANT TO GO HOME?

YOU'RE IN THE MIDDLE OF THE WORLD NOW
    BABY!

DO YOU KNOW HOW MUCH I LOVE YOU?

WHAT DOES IT MEAN
IF YOU READ ALL THIS
POETRY AND DON'T KNOW
IT'S ABOUT YOU

THIS IS THE PARTY
FANTASY. TO DISSOLVE INTO
EVERYONE ELSE FALLING
INTO EACH OTHER, INTO
ONE LUMP, ONE DRUNK
LUMP, ALL MELDING AND
MESHING AT THE SAME
TEMPO, THIS UNORIGINALITY,
THIS AMBIGUITY, THE TURNED
DOWN LIGHTS AT A PARTY,
THE MUSIC THAT BEATS
UNTIL IT NUMBS YOU OUT,
THE HAZE. THERE IS A
CERTAIN MESHING I'M
LOOKING FOR WITH
MYSELF. I'M TRYING TO
HOLD MYSELF WHILE ALSO
BEING HELD. I JUST

CAN'T TELL WHOSE ARMS
ARE HOLDING ME. I DON'T
KNOW WHOSE THEY ARE.
IT'S LATE AND I'M
TIRED AND I HAVEN'T
GOTTEN ENOUGH SLEEP,
MY MOM TELLS ME THIS
IS THE REASON FOR MY
SADNESS. I KNOW THAT
THIS ISN'T TRUE, BUT
I LET HER HAVE IT. I OPEN
MY DOOR TO FIND AN
EMPTINESS I HAVE GONE
HOME WITH. I DON'T LIKE
BRINGING STRANGERS
HOME. I HAVE DISCOVERED
THIS IN THE CAR RIDES
HOME NOW. I HAVE

DISCOVERED IAM FEELING
TERRIBLY SAD. IAM ~~FEELING~~
TERRIBLY ALONE. ~~IAM FEELING~~
IAM FEELING TERRIBLY
ALONE. I AM FEELING
UNHELD.

IT IS LATE. IT IS ALMOST 1 AM.
I AM TIRED AND EVERYONE IS
ASLEEP. I AM TRYING TO
FORM A KIND OF CORRESPONDANCE
BETWEEN MY HEART AND MY
SOUL. I AM TRYING TO BE
VERY CAREFUL WITH IT. I AM
UN COMFORTABLE AND AM
FEELING EMBARRASSED
AND TOO LONG. I AM NEVER
SURE HOW TO END THESE.
I DON'T ~~SETTLE~~ SETTLE
WELL WITH THE IDEA
THAT A DIARY ENTRY IS
FINITE. I REALIZE THAT
TIME, BY NOW, IS PLAYING
OUT IN A BACKGROUND
THAT I WOULD WISH TO AVOID.
I AM SEEING THAT MY ~~IS~~
MEMORIES ARE ALL

EXISTING IN THIS ONE MOMENT.
I CANNOT THINK OF THE
MOMENTNESS AS ANYTHING
OTHER THAN PAINFULLY RAW.
I HOPE YOU READ THESE AS
CONTINUUMS AND NEVER
AS FACTS, MAYBE AS TRUTHS,
AND FOR SURE ALL OF MY
BEING ON ONE PAGE.
I HOPE YOU KNOW THAT I
AM LYING BESIDE MYSELF,
IN THE SAME BED. I AM
TRYING TO GET VERY
SMALL. I AM TRYING TO FEEL
MY SOUL AGAINST MY
BONES. I AM TRYING TO
CURL UP AND FEEL
MYSELF GROWING; I AM
TRY TO FIND THE ~~RELAT~~
RELATIONSHIP BETWEEN

FEELING VERY OLD AND VERY
YOUNG. I AM TRYING TO
EXPLAIN TO YOU THAT I AM
ALL AT ONCE A FADED
YELLOW, WAVES CRASHING
INTO THE SHORE, AND HOURS
OF THE MORNING JUST
BEFORE EVERYONE ELSE
WAKES UP, WHERE WHAT
SEEMS LIKE A NEW DAY
IS A DAY THAT IS ALREADY
VERY OLD, A DAY THAT
HAS FOLDED IN AND
OUT OF ITSELF MANY
TYMES OVER.

I am sorry if
these letters are
rambling,
but I am trying
to, above all,
figure out who
these letters are for.

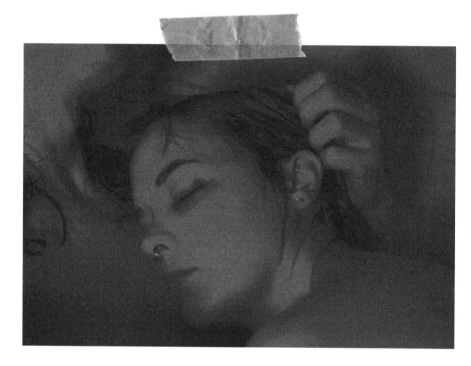

"hunger"

this body is a nuisance.

its needs

its desires

its desperate clawing at

its own emptiness.

i long to think my way out of

physicality.

to think myself out of existence.

survival is brutal;

being is demanding.

sleep, eat, breathe,

cry, scream, tense,

release.

god, if only i could.

does water ever want?

does the sky seek fulfillment?

and why should i?

and why should i?

and why should i?

the only salvation
is imagination

MY BODY HURTS AND ACHES WITH THE THE THOUGHT OF AN END
THIS BODY, THE SAME BODY THAT IS NAKED IN FRONT OF ME
WHISPERS STOP EATING (STOP LIVING)
SO THAT EVERYONE ELSE COULD LIVE A LITTLE LIGHTER
WHAT WOULD HAPPEN IF THIS BODY WEREN'T HERE?

WOULD MY DOG GO TO MY BED TO TRY TO FIND IT
OR DOES HE KNOW IT HAD BEEN LOST FOR A WHILE

DOES HE SMELL THE BLOOD, SWEAT, AND TEARS
THAT BELONGED TO MY MOTHER ON THE DAY MY BODY WAS BORN
DOES HE SENSE THE SPACE THAT IS NOW EMPTY
BETWEEN MY BODY AND HER BODY
AND HOW I'VE BEEN TRYING TO ~~CRW~~ CRAWL CLOSER
TO THE LETTER SHE WROTE ME IN PRESCHOOL
WHICH IS SO MUCH SMALLER
THAN MY BODY
AND HER BODY
AND OUR BODIES

DOES MY DOG KNOW HIS SCENT ON MY BODY
DOES HE KNOW THE DIFFERENCE BETWEEN
WHAT IS MINE
AND WHAT IS HIS
DOES HE KNOW THAT THIS BODY, THIS SAME BODY
WALKS ALONE AT NIGHT

HAUNTED BY OTHER DOGS WHO DRIVE LAMBORGHINIS
THAT GRAZE BY # IT ~~AND CALL IT THEIR BABY~~
CALL IT THEIR ~~BABY~~

WHEN I WAS TEN
MY MOM TAUGHT ME
TO KEEP ONE KEY IN BETWEEN MY RING
FINGER AND MIDDLE FINGER
SO I COULD STOP ANY DOGS WHO MIGHT TRY TO PET ME

BUT I WISH SHE WOULD'VE TOLD ME
I AM ALREADY

WALKING VIOLENCE

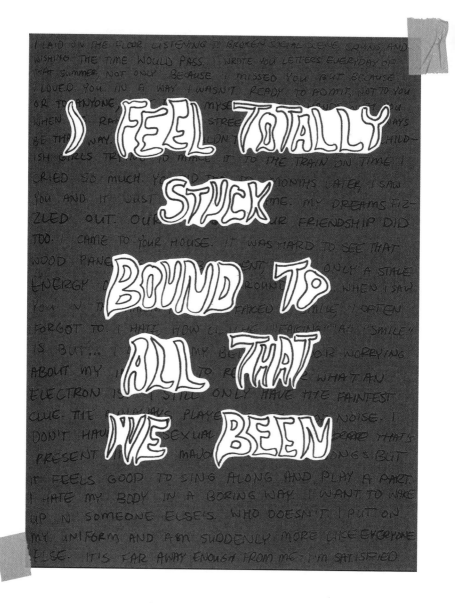

I LAID ON THE FLOOR LISTENING TO BROKEN SOCIAL SCENE CRYING AND WISHING THE TIME WOULD PASS. I WROTE YOU LETTERS EVERYDAY OF THAT SUMMER NOT ONLY BECAUSE I MISSED YOU BUT BECAUSE I LOVED YOU IN A WAY I WASN'T READY TO ADMIT, NOT TO YOU OR TO ANYONE, NOT EVEN MYSELF. ... YOU WHEN I RA... STREE... ...AYS BE THI... WAY. ...ULDN'T ... CHILD- ISH GIRLS TRY... TO MAKE IT TO THE TRAIN ON TIME I CRIED SO MUCH. YO... TO... MONTHS LATER, I SAW YOU AND IT JUST ... ME. MY DREAMS FIZ- ZLED OUT. OUR ... UR FRIENDSHIP DID TOO. I CAME TO YOUR HOUSE. IT WAS HARD TO SEE THAT WOOD PANE... ...ENT, ONLY A STALE ENERGY ... ROUND... WHEN I SAW YOU V TH... FACED ... MILE I OFTEN FORGOT TO I HATE HOW LL... FAKI... A "SMILE" IS BUT... I ... MY BE... OR WORRYING ABOUT MY ... TO R... WHAT AN ELECTRON IS... I STILL ONLY HAVE THE FAINTEST CLUE THE ... PLAYE... NOISE. I DON'T HAV... SEXUAL ... ...RE THAT'S PRESENT ... MAJO... ...NGS BUT IT FEELS GOOD TO SING ALONG AND PLAY A PART. I HATE MY BODY IN A BORING WAY. I WANT TO WAKE UP IN SOMEONE ELSE'S. WHO DOESN'T. I PUT ON MY UNIFORM AND AM SUDDENLY MORE LIKE EVERYONE ELSE. IT IS FAR AWAY ENOUGH FROM ME - I'M SATISFIED

I FEEL TOTALLY STUCK BOUND TO ALL THAT I'VE BEEN

when you're young you wanna trust

Lust is Lust is Lust is Lust
Lust is salty
Lust is sweet
   doesn't Last, Lust is selfish

it is hard to write and smoke at the same time because i
do both with my left hand. the people on the beach below
me look so tiny. there is one very small square shaped cloud
ahead of me and the rest of the sky is vast. the sun streaks
the air with milky fog and in this moment right now i am
so grateful to be laying alone on the blue blanket that has
collected sand from so many different places along this
coast i get to call my home. i am inextricably tied to
here. everywhere that pushes me, everywhere that pulls
me, always leaves my toes in a collection of millions of
rock sediments. the sea is white on the shore. i am so
happy to be alive. this moment is perfect, i am exactly where
i want to be. i am surrounded by grass that reminds me
of eyelashes. there is a cloud above me that looks like a
feather and a hole at the top of it that i envisioned my
soul lifting up through. everything will be pink soon. what have
i done to deserve this space all around me? i smell salt. my
favorite feeling in the world is being tired from the sun. there
are so many different ways to be in love and i am so grateful
that i have the capacity to hold it all inside me. i find so
much comfort in the sea, the Pacific has witnessed so many
experiences throughout my life. for the first time, i know i
have learned that solitude has so much to offer. everything
that helps me to grow is good. i haven't felt a peace like
this in a very long time. i am free. i am one freckle on the
face of the earth. glowing and shining and turning and whole.

   i am whole all alone sitting here in love with the
     solitude i have blessed to claim as mine.
           been   with
my favorite polka dot leggings have holes in them now.
the sea is a rainbow. i love every color.

remember this state of being. you always come home to it.
  today is february 23.

EVERYWHERE I TURN, I SEE
THEM. THEM, NOT THE
PERSON, BUT THE LIGHT,
FLASHES OF NEON, THE
LYRICS I SO OFTEN
OVERLOOKED - MORE AND
MORE DO MOMENTS
OCCUR WHERE EVERYTHING
SLOWS TO A STOP. ~~THE~~
THESE UNEXPLAINABLE
FEELINGS START TO
SWELL IN MY STOMACH
AT THE THOUGHT OF
THESE MOMENTS OCCURRING
AGAIN - THESE MOMENTS
OF LOVE.

I HAVE BEEN SAD A LOT
LATELY ABOUT THE
INEVITABLE LOSS OF TIME.
I HAVE A LUMP IN MY
THROAT JUST THINKING
ABOUT IT - SHANE'S 5TH
GRADE YEARBOOK PHOTO,
CARM~~EN~~ CRYING ON HER
13TH BIRTHDAY ~~A SURREALISM~~
- SURREALISM. I DO NOT
THINK I HAVE KNOWN A
TIME IN MY LIFE WHERE
I HAVEN'T FELT A SENSE
OF LOSS, OR A FEELING
OF WATCHING, ~~OF DISCONN~~
OF DISCONNECT: SOMETIMES
WHEN PEOPLE GET SAD

AROUND ME AND I GO TO
COMFORT THEM, I CAN'T
HELP BUT SMILE, NOT
BECAUSE I THINK THEIR
PAIN IS FUNNY, BUT
BECAUSE I AM SO
ENTHRALLED BY THE
POWER OF LONGING,
AND THE THINGS WE SAY
THAT ARE EXTRAORDINARY.
SOMETIMES WHEN I AM
WITH FRIENDS, EITHER
THEY POINT OUT, OR I
BECOME AWARE OF HOW
LONG I'VE BEEN STARING
AT THEM, FASCINATED BY
JUST THE EXPRESSION OF

THEIR THINKING (LOOKING
~~TO~~ THROUGH A CAMERA).

I REALIZE THAT MAYBE
ALL ALONG, MY FEELINGS
FOR BOYS WERE ALWAYS
THE SAME AS MY
FEELINGS FOR PEOPLE
IN GENERAL: IF I AM
GIVEN A MOMENT, ANY
MOMENT WITH ANY PERSON
THAT OUTLASTS THE MOMENT
ITSELF AND CASCADES INTO
A FLURRY IN MY CHEST
AND INTO PAGES IN MY DIARY
-A FEELING OF INFINITY AND
OF EVERYTHING HAPPENING
AT ONCE - I COULD LOVE

THEM, THIS LOVE BEING
PLATONIC OR ROMANTIC
AND EVERYTHING IN BE
BETWEEN.
  RAEGAN'S BIRTHDAY
WAS ABOUT A WEEK AGO,
AND I HAVE BEEN
STRUGGLING WITH HER
PRESENT, BECAUSE NO
MATTER WHAT I TRY, SHE
WILL NEVER KNOW HOW
MUCH I LOVE HER. I HAVE
TROUBLE HUGGING HER
EVEN, TROUBLE LOOKING HER
IN THE EYE. I AM ALWAYS
AFRAID I MAY NOT EXPRESS
MY LOVE ENOUGH, THAT
SHE WILL NOT UNDERSTAND

HOW MUCH SHE MEANS
TO ME, HOW I MIGHT'VE
ESCAPED MYSELF WITHOUT
HER... THERE IS NO WAY
TO EXPRESS THAT. SHE
AND I ARE EVERYTHING
HAPPENING IN THE
UNIVERSE ENTANGLED INTO
TWO PEOPLE. OUR
UNIVERSE IS SUCH A SAFE
ONE. IT IS JUST US. TIME
ERASES ITSELF AND IS
REBORN ONE THOUSAND
TIMES TO MEET US IN
THESE MOMENTS. HOW MAGICAL.

(HOW TO FALL IN LOVE:

RECORD THESE MOMENTS
IN YOUR MIND, REPLAY
THEM OVER AND OVER IN
YOUR HEAD, ASSOCIATE
THEM WITH THIS LYRIC IN
THIS SONG, PROJECT HOW
YOU FEEL ONTO THE OTHER
PERSON SO YOU CAN
FEEL IT BACK, BASK
IN THE FLUTTER OF YOUR
HEART, TRY TO CONVINCE
YOURSELF THAT FEELING
IS ENOUGH)

ALL OF THOSE MOMENTS
WITH HIM THAT HE LATER
DENIED - DON'T THINK FOR
A SECOND THAT THEY DID
NOT HAPPEN. YOU GIVE
SO MUCH LOVE THAT YOU
MISTAKE YOUR OWN FOR
THE LOVE OF OTHERS.
THE VIGNETTES YOU HAVE
EDITED TOGETHER HAVE
BECOME YOUR FAVORITE
MOVIES - HOW COULD YOU
BLAME YOURSELF?

YOU ARE
EVERY COLOR
I CAN'T NAME

FOTR POWERED BY Xbox 360
The Princess Bride
Carbon Leaf
DENVER FILM SOCIETY
Rain or Shine/ Doors at 6:30pm
TUESDAY JUNE 30, 2009 DUSK
GENERAL ADMISSION   TICKET PRICE

KS082A
A0630
9980
082A
AD
PRICE $10.00 CONV FEE $0.50
Admit One
NERAL
MIT
29/2009

Ritzy Picturehouse, Brixton
2 Jan 2013   £0.00
ife of Pi 2D   B3
creen   Cert   Time
creen 4   PG   18:00
Ref: K4NRN9

Duke of York's
ct 2011   £8.00
ncholia   GA
en   Cert   Time
en 1   15   20:00
Ref: MN8YKQ

Phoenix Picturehouse, Oxford
13 Nov 2011   £8.50
The Future   GA
Screen   Cert   Time
Screen 2   12A   13:00
Ref: FHZHVP

Picturehouse, Brixton
2013   £9.50
Pi 2D   B4
Cert   Time
4   PG   18:00
Ref: K4NRN9

Sorry I had too g

love you xx

CU
L8R!
XO
XO

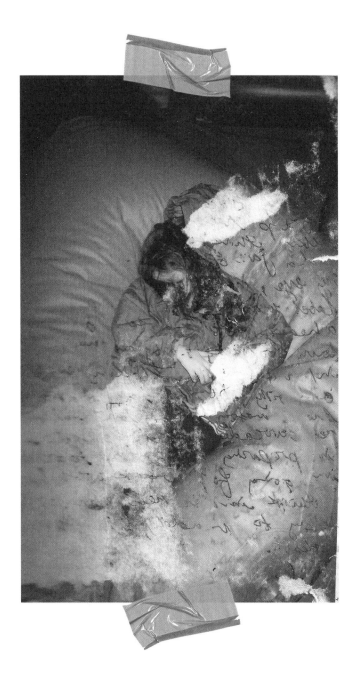

ever since you left i have dreams of never being able to reach you. Us living separate lives, in a different world. with only the feeling of a knife in my stomach. A funeral for something that can only be told or felt in the heart.

AT WHAT POINT DOES MY
BODY BECOME CLOTHES

WHEN CAN I SLIP IT ON
SLIP IT OFF

AT WHAT POINT DO I GET
UP OFF MY KNEES

(I REALIZE THIS IS NOT MY
OWN DOING)

(BUT STILL)

AT WHAT POINT DOES IT
BECOME CLOTHES

AT WHAT POINT
DOES MY BODY
BECOME MY CHOICE

I TRIED TO FILL THIS EMPTY
SPACE WITH GOOD WORDS BUT
I AM STILL EMPTY

IN A DREAM
I FORGAVE YOU BUT I CAN'T RIGHT NOW

(PLEASE DON'T TRY TO CONTACT ME)

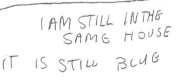

I AM STILL IN THE
SAME HOUSE

IT IS STILL BLUE

on the third day I lose the color of
my skin and my eyes darken

on the fourth day I denounce my body.
motionless, I let my fingernails coil and my
head rests until I fall mute.

on the fifth day I eat you in my sleep.
my jaw weakens
you sit inside my stomach and I break my
arms trying to reach you

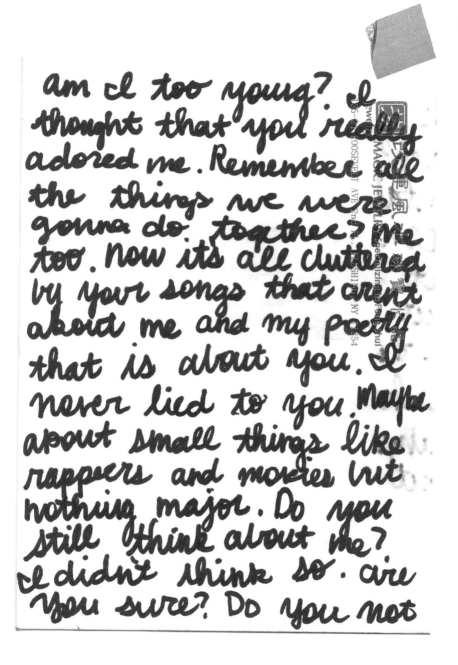

am I too young? I
thought that you really
adored me. Remember all
the things we were
gonna do together? Me
too. Now its all cluttered
by your songs that aren't
about me and my poetry
that is about you. I
never lied to you. Maybe
about small things like
rappers and movies but
nothing major. Do you
still think about me?
I didn't think so. are
you sure? Do you not

feel things? Sorry that was rude. But honestly? Fine. You used to take photographs of me. I'd tell you how much I hated it when people talked bad about the rain and you agreed. Learning to love you less is hard. I want to tell you things. Guess I'll never know. But I am fine now.

I treat my
memory like a
fire and burn my
hands trying to
put you out

The Dumb Cunt Exegesis of Love Letters Once Considered No Less than Divine

It's so fucked up
that i was thanking you for being nice to me
maybe the happy times don't exist in the blank spaces
if i can read these letters like history
im not looking back for a plot

11/11/2015

THE DUMB CUNT EXEGESIS OF LOVE
LETTERS SENT PAST MIDNIGHT

THE DUMB CUNT EXEGESIS OF OH
FUCK I TOLD ~~XXXXXX~~ THAT I LOVE

THE DUMB CUNT EXEGESIS OF A
MEETING BETWEEN MYSELF AND
YOUR MOTHER WHO WANTS US
TO GET MARRIED SO THAT I CAN
BEAR HER GRANDCHILDREN

THE DUMB CUNT EXEGESIS IS A PHRASE
I AM CLINGING TO IN ORDER TO MASK
THE FACT THAT IT IS IMPOSSIBLE TO
WRITE POETRY ABOUT YOU

11/11/2015

Historiography — study of how history has been written —

First Quest for Historical Jesus
late 18th — 1906 (@ time of Protestant Reformation)
Enlightenment 18th — Darwin's origin of Species — ideas of HUMANS came about & how

HERMAN SAMUEL REIMARUS
↳ political messianic figure who was not famous / listened to in his time ɜ published post-humously

DAVID STRAUSS (1808 - 1874)
—life of jesus critically examined
Gospels to him, weren't historical —
they were myths

ERNAST RENAN (1823 - 1892)
Works in Paris — wrote a romantic biography —
Made arguments about how Miracles rationally occurred

JOHANNES WEISS (1892) — Jesus preach should be understand in context of Jewish Apocalypsm

HOW TO FEEL ABOUT: A NOUN

ADV.	NOUN	IN
~~STORMY~~	~~DEATH~~	~~JUNE~~
~~POINTLESS~~	~~KISS~~	~~JULY~~
~~STICKY~~	~~SKINSHIP~~	~~BED~~
~~WET~~	~~VISIT~~	~~DREAM~~
~~OLD~~	~~TALK~~	~~STRANGERS HOME~~
~~COLORFUL~~	~~WALK~~	~~LUSH GRASS~~
~~SOFT~~	~~FUCK~~	~~PURPLE SKY~~
~~QUIET~~	~~MEAL~~	~~FOG OR MIST~~

HOW TO FEEL · ABOUT A

~~STORMY~~ POINTLESS TALK IN A STRANGERS HOME,

OR A COLORFUL MEAL UNDER A PURPLE SKY?

OR AN OLD VISITOR FROM JULY?

A ~~WET~~ WALK IN JUNE

A STICKY KISS IN LUSH GRASS

A SOFT DEATH in a DREAM

QUIET SUNSHINE IN ~~BED~~

A STORMY FUCK OF FOG

---

it smelled like a raindrop
but tasted like a teardrop

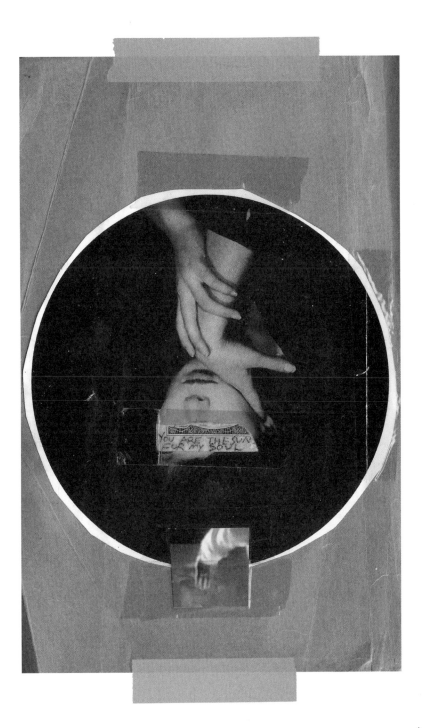

I THREW AWAY THE BOTTLE OF
BEER I WAS HIDING

(NO CLUE WHY IT WAS THERE IN
THE ~~FIRST~~ PLACE)

I CAN'T HOLD MYSELF WITHOUT CRYING
BUT ITS DIFFERENT REASONS NOW.

ITS BETTER REASONS NOW

ITS THE PART OF FEELING THANGS
FOR THE FIRST TIME NOW.

I WONDER HOW MANY NIGHTS I
DIPPED THROUGH TO GET TO THAT ONE.

WILL I EVER FEEL THE SAME AWAY
AGAIN, THE WAY I DID, THAT NIGHT?

DO U THINK IF WE STAY UP ALL NIGHT
TIME WILL GO SLOWER?

SOMEWHERE THERES A FRECKLE IN
A CROWD AND SHES ABOUT TO COME
OF AGE

MOM JUST CAME IN I SHUT HER
OUT REAL QUICK

WHY WOULD I DO THAT? WHY DID
YOU DO THAT?

I THREW AWAY THE BOTTLE
OF BEER I WAS HIDING

~~I'M LYING DOWN ON MY ROOM ON~~
~~THE FLOOR I WISH I COULD TELL~~
~~YOU EVERYTHING AND THAT~~
~~WHILE MUSIC DOWNSTAIRS~~
~~BURST SO LOUD~~

IM LYING DOWN ON THE FLOOR
IN MY ROOM I WISH I COULD TELL YOU
EVERYTHING. ~~AND THAT THE MUSIC~~

THINKING ABOUT HOLDING IT IN.
SOME KIND OF SURGING WET
IT
WHATEVER
IM SURE YOU'VE GOT SOME KIND OF
IDEA ABOUT IT NOW
BUT THAT DOESN'T MAKE IT YOURS
IT, IS THE UNOWNED IT
ONLY SOMETIMES HELD
STILL
POINTING A BLANK FACE AT
ALL THE OTHER VIBRATIONS
INVITING
THIS MUST BE ONE OF THOSE
AWKWARD MOMENTS
~~THE~~ WHEN YOU CANT READ
YOUR OWN HANDWRITTING.
IT CAN PROVE EMBARRASSINGLY
DIFFICULT TO PUT A BRACELET
~~X~~ ON ALL BY YOUR SELF.

I HOPE SOMEDAY
        YOU CAN FORGIVE ME

BUT PLEASE   UNDERSTAND
      I CAN'T
            FORGIVE ME
      RIGHT NOW

I HAVE BEEN BUSY GREIVING ALL
THE PEOPLE I USED TO BE

In the beauty that
was circling in her rounded shoulders
the innocence sliding down through her collarbones,
pouring pure grace down in the deep depths of her breasts
outlining her waist with the intuition with which she foretold
can you blame her, as you ~~watch~~ imagine lust hugging each side of her hips
and her legs, with which she walks as the confidence within them exudes
she has eyes deeper than the oceans and seas
her skin reminding you of buttercream and caramels
and best of all—her smile,
which could bring a raging city to its knees.
she is beautiful, intelligent, skilled and graceful,
she is every woman, girl and child.
she does not lack a thing and has power to do the greatest of things
she is my mother and yours. she is ~~my sister~~ all the sisters among us
and the daughters which we love. she is the soul mate
that holds us until we feel peace at night.
~~do~~ you agree, don't you? so then why have you told her she is not
beautiful or serene. why have you used her. and dumped her next to filth.
why do you think she is inferior? why do you look down upon her when she is
confident in what she does? why can't she wear what she wants, and
why is it that it is always you that stops her. why
do you not have faith in her, your lack of it,
showing how faithless you are in yourself.
Remember—she is Woman—
and the day she begins to believe all the
lies you tell her, is the day
the <u>END</u> will surely begin

THERE'S A PLACE TUCKED AWAY DEEP IN MY BONES THAT FEELS LIKE SACRED GROUNDS AND ANCIENT LIVES. I WANT TO GO THERE BUT THIS WORLD IS PULLING ME TO STAY. WHEN I THINK OF THE LIFETIMES I'VE SEEN AND EXPERIENCED, EACH VERY TRUE TO MY SOUL BUT UNDOUBTEDLY UNKNOWN TO MY MIND, MY WORRIES FEEL LIKE PEBBLES THROWN OUT AT SEA. THEY FEEL SMALL AND EASILY CARRIED AWAY BY THE CURRENTS BUT THIS WORLD TELLS ME TO WORRY. TO WORRY IS TO CARE. ANOTHER LIMITING BELIEF SWIRLING AROUND IN MY HEAD. MY MOTHER TELLS ME THAT THE UNIVERSE ALWAYS PROVIDES AND I BELIEVE HER, MOST NIGHTS. TONIGHT I AM FAR FROM WORRIED BUT I AM NOT SURE IF ANYTHING IS REAL. ALL MY MEMORIES FEEL LIKE SMOKE AND GLASS MIRRORS AND I'M NOT SURE IF ANYTHING I'VE FELT IN THE PAST IS REAL EITHER. THAT SCARES ME BUT IT MOSTLY MAKES ME SAD. TO THINK ALL MY MEMORIES ONE DAY WILL BECOME DUST MAKES ME FEARLESS BUT ALSO FILLS ME WITH A DEEP SENSE OF POINTLESSNESS.

Mother —

in any situation, I collapse into myself
the lining of your eyes justifies nothing but
the composure of my concrete skin
when they undertook your organs, did you reject
your skin? were you ever so unkind and absent
and did you regret drinking your heart the way
you are trained to do when they assert your
innocence into the way you bend at the knee
and worship the feeling of god inbetween your
hands, and what did you see rupture when you
sought me bloom from your own skin? what did
you see all those times when you stood alone, unable
to recognize your own breaking body?

I MOVED OUTSIDE TO FIND THAT THE
SAME YELLOW FLOWERS I TOLD
YOU ABOUT ARE GROWING IN OUR
BACKYARD NOW. SOME OF THESE
THINGS ARE PURE COMFORTS.
THEY ARE REMINDERS THAT
THERE IS ENOUGH QUIET
PEACE IN THE WORLD TO WILL
YOURSELF TO STAY ALIVE: YOU
JUST HAVE TO LOOK AROUND AND
THERE IT IS. YOU DON'T HAVE
TO WISH FOR IT, IT IS ALREADY
THERE. ~~YOU DON'T~~ THIS IS A
SIMPLE ENOUGH FACT
FOR ME TO BELIEVE IN.
I AM TRYING TO FIND A
COMPLICATED BEAUTY IN THE
SIMPLE. I'M EXPLAINING
TO MYSELF SOME THINGS
CAN JUST BE AND

THAT BEING IS A FACT. THERE
ARE LESSONS I AM SURE WILL
NOT BECOME CONCRETE FOR
ME FOR A LONG TIME,
BUT I CAN STILL TRUST THERE
IS A LOT MORE GOOD CLOSER
TO YOU THAN MAY SEEM.
AND THE PURE GOOD YOU ARE
SEARCHING FOR IS USUALLY
YOURSELF, OR YOUR CHILDSELF,
WHO IS NOT AS FAR AS YOU
THINK. THERE IS A
COMFORT I AM TRYING
TO FIND IN MY
SMALLNESS, MY GROWING,
IN EVERYTHING I DO NOT
KNOW, THERE IS SOMETHING
THAT IS HOLDING ME ABOUT
THE SMALLNESS OF
FLOWERS IN THE WIND.
MAYBE IT IS BECAUSE IT
REMINDS ME OF A QUIET
I CANNOT NAME.

I WISH I
COULD TELL
YOU WHAT
IT FEELS
LIKE
TO HEAR
ONLY EARTH

I HOPE YOU KNOW
THIS FEELING
ALREADY.

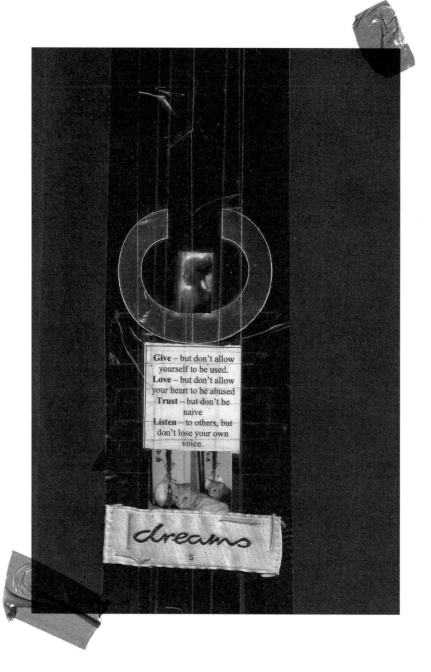

Give – but don't allow yourself to be used.
Love – but don't allow your heart to be abused
Trust – but don't be naive
Listen – to others, but don't lose your own voice.

dreams

LEARNING TO BE ALIVE IS AN INCREDIBLY AMBITIOUS UNDERTAKING.

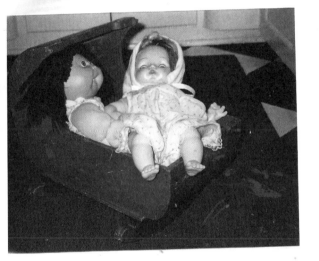

LEARNING TO BE ALIVE IS AN INCREDIBLY AMBITIOUS UNDERTAKING.

I AM TRYING TO TEACH HER ALL THE WAYS HER BODY HAS BROKEN AND ALL THE WAYS IT WILL HEAL
I AM TRYING TO HUG HER IN A WAY THAT IS NOT TOO TIGHT BUT JUST THERE
I AM TRYING TO LEARN THAT I CAN JUST BE THERE
AND THAT JUST BEING THERE
IS A HOLY PRACTICE.

SOMETIMES WHEN I AM BROKEN
I HEAR HER WHISPERING.
QUIET AND RAGE EXIST IN YOU AT ONCE AND THIS DOES NOT MAKE YOU WEAK
IT MAKES YOU LIKE THE RAIN.

OF COURSE
THE WORLD EXISTS
OUTSIDE ME
BUT RIGHT NOW
THERE IS A LOT OF PAIN
I'M TRYING TO RESOLVE
~~THANK YOU~~
(~~PLEASE LET ME,~~)
~~THANK YOU~~
THANK YOU FOR
LETTING ME

space.
   space that adapts to the edges and sharp turns
of an (your)
   ever-changing, ever blooming. identity.

There is something... sacred.
                about our space

something true and bitter shifts inside us when we
realize we've become mature. pine trees and our
beloved space are mere supportive stilts we no
longer need.

REMINDERS: YOU NEED TO BE ALONE VERY OFTEN BUT IF YOU STAY ALONE YOU GET DEPRESSED. PEOPLE GIVE YOU LIFE, ENERGY & STRENGTH. WHEN YOU GET TOO PERSONAL ON THE INTERNET YOU ALMOST ALWAYS REGRET IT AFTER. MORNINGS ARE YOUR TIME, YOU DON'T NEED TO HATE YOURSELF FOR THE THINGS YOU CAN'T CONTROL, LIKE THE WAY YOUR BODY FEELS DRAINED IN THE EVENINGS. YOU WAKE UP & CHARGE WITH THE SUN. THERE ARE SO MANY KINDS OF LOVE IN THE WORLD, NOT TOO MENTION THE **
WARMTH YOU ALREADY HAVE **
** DIP INTO THESE FEELINGS OF CALM. MAKE LISTS OF WHAT YOU HAVE AND NOT JUST WHAT YOU HAVE TO DO. GOOD WORK TAKES TIME & PATIENCE BUT BEST WORK COMES FAST WHEN YOU (I) ARE LEAST EXPECTING IT. TRUST IT. IT IS LIKE LOVE, AND YOU MIGHT GET HURT. ** ** * * ** * **

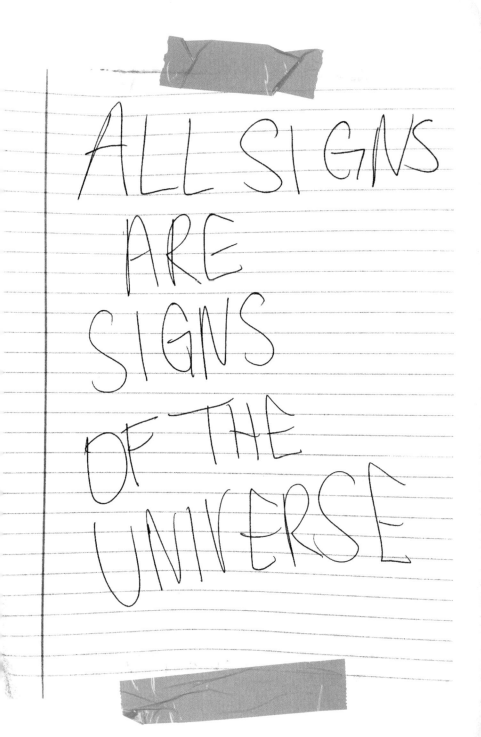

ALL SIGNS ARE SIGNS OF THE UNIVERSE

SURVIVAL IS A **LOOP**, It hurts and we return to some learning points when we dont want to. It hurts but it helps make us who we are — even though | it is NOT all we are. |

Now, more than ever, I think about the frustration I feel, the dissassociation (lol, sp), the hopelessness, the audacity of the hope I feel when I feel it (most of the time on good days).... I also think about endurance, and how the love I feel for the other queers & other ppl of color & immigrants & sick kids, all of us, how endurance, love - it is our inheritence, and we have jobs to do, and we are good at it even when the world is inhospitable. we're here to leave evidence, to prove we dont need proof of our humanity and complexity from ppl not here furs - we are better than them regardless - IN SPITE OF IT. IN THE FACE OF IT!! So many people have done everything they could to get us here. There debt and love and hope in our BONES. we carry it with us. now more than ever I want to translate all of it, all that power, push as much as I can, to do what little I can, to make things a little more endurable for someone else. because I know it matters. I matter to people, and people matter to me. I have hope for us. I will not let despair kill my potential. theres time for that when I'm dead. which will happen eventually. dont have to rush it. nobody said it was easy, any of this. the older I get, the more I see. the more frustrated, more confused,.... but I also see how absolutely essential even & especially the small good things are. When big things fail & shatter we're left with small shards. given enough patience, endurance, persistence, you can make something out of all those broken parts. you can start all over, make things better -differently- more sustainable. you must try. you dont even need to think you'll be the one to really fix everything. you just need to do enough work to ease the burden for someone else, who is also hurting because of these shards, and who is as committed as you are. we're never alone.
we have to take care of each other.

PAY ATTENTION
HONOR TENDERNESS
& NO MATTER
WHAT— DO NOT
LOSE FAITH

GO AS FAR AS
YOU CAN
ITS IN YOUR
HEAD ALREADY
LET IT OUT

✓ nothing is just
in your head

everything is in
your ~~head~~
instincts
— DURGA

↑ POST IT SPELLS THAT SAVE MY
LIFE EVERY MORNING.

WHAT BINDS ME HERE?
WHO IS DESERVING OF LOVE,
STRENGTH, RAGE, HOPE? (we miss you
mark aguhar.)
HOW DO YOU ENDURE THE
UNENDURABLE AND STILL FIND WAYS
TO LOVE, WITHOUT FEELING FOOLISH FOR IT?

hope vs. desire vs. optimism
..... where does endurance
and action metamorphize (sp?)
dreams into reality, into if
not now then soon?

when you decide you can't go
on as it stands. so, now, right now.
noooooooooouw.

hope is not a dream or an escape, it is an
actionable force, something that can move
mountains, makes sure people never die
(the people who we lost push us forward)
hope can burn everything in its path, break
down doors (an axe in an emergency—Solnit)
and makes mothers move trucks with their
bare hands. desire gets you there. desire
is complicated - can contain rage, betrayal,
hurt. history, family, sisterhood. love. when
you have desire you have a burning force
you have to endure and channel or
be humiliated by what was possible that
you were to afraid to run after. run towards.
it costs. survival is expensive. again and
again hope will feel like its not enough. again
and again you may fall short. but you have to endure to see even small changes, to
fail upwards, to force the world to treat you differently. its awful, its not easy, and it is
the only thing worth doing - to try to make all of this more endurable, to not feel alone,
to make sure someone, somewhere, feels love. to know its possible, to know you have to be here.

LETTER FOR THE LITTLE QUEER GIRL IN THE MIDDLE OF THE NIGHT

WHAT IS YOUR WAY OF PROTECTION?
WHAT DO YOU HOLD ON TO IN THE
MIDDLE OF THE NIGHT TO KEEP
YOU WARM?

WHAT KEEPS YOU UP AT NIGHT?
WHAT SECRETS DO YOU KEEP
FROM YOURSELF?

DOES IT FEEL GOOD?
DOES IT FEEL GOOD TO HAVE THE
LITTLE SECRET WITH YOU?
DO YOU CARE FOR IT?
DO YOU CARE FOR IT HOW A
MOTHER CARES FOR HER CHILD?
IS YOUR QUEERNESS LIKE MINE?

DOES IT WHISPER TO YOU?
DO YOU HOLD IT?
SOMETIMES, IN THIS SPECIAL
TIMES, DOES IT HOLD YOU?

DO YOU KNOW IT IS OKAY?
DO YOU KNOW IT IS OKAY TO BE
QUEER?

THE SECRET LANGUAGE
OF EMPTY SPACES.
WE WILL HOLD THEM, TOGETHER.
WE WILL HOLD HANDS, TOGETHER.
WE WILL FIND ALL THE WAYS WE
CAN FOLD AND UNFOLD. BE
BORN, AND UNBORN, AND REBORN.

WHEN I AM BROKEN AND
BETRAYED, I PRAY THAT YOU
WILL HOLD ME WHEN I CANNOT
HOLD YOU.
WHEN I AM BROKEN AND
BETRAYED,
I PRAY YOU WILL REMIND ME
BROKEN IS A WAY OF QUEERNESS.

THERE IS NOT ONLY ONE WAY
TO ~~B~~ MEND YOUR PIECES.

I HOPE GOD WILL TELL YOU TO
REMIND ME THAT UNKNOWNESS
IS A WAY OF QUEERNESS TOO.
AND THAT, WE WILL EXPLORE, TOGETHER,
THE UNCHARTED TERRITORIES AND
BROKEN TREES.
AND WE WILL PROMISE EACH OTHER.
WE WILL FIND NEW WAYS OF
MENDING THEM.

PLEASE WHISPER TO ME,
FROM THE CORNERS OF THE
WORLD:

YOU WILL FIND ALL OF THE
NEW WAYS TO MEND.
YOU WILL FIND ALL OF THE
NEWS WAYS TO THROW.
YOU WILL FIND ALL OF THE NEWS
WAYS TO LOVE.

147

eyes are closed. first focus on breath, inhale as deeply as i can - hold it. exhale through my mouth. i tried to count my breaths. one two three. second focus on the heat coming from the shower head, focus on my skin's temperature rising. i sat down on the floor and leaned against the wall. i closed my eyes again. i re-focused on my breath. third i focus on the sensation of hot water tapping on my body. i focus on the way my skin felt on the tiles of the ground. i re-focus on my breath. fourth i focus on the sound of the shower and the muffled chatter in the kitchen. the smell of where i sat was sweet, like shampoo and flowers. i thought of the last time i was on the bathroom floor and let it pass through me. that time was an accident. this time was intentional. i turn my body so my face is under the shower head and i concentrate again on the physical sensation of hot water raining over my eyes closed. i opened my eyes and observe the colors around me. first i saw light orange, my gaze shifts to blue and i stared for awhile. it was dark blue but it was bright. i shift to the pink tile wall but it was not the most pleasant pink so i looked down at the pale green cap on a shampoo bottle. i like that color. i stood up and again turned my attention to my breath. i lost count so long ago. my towel is a dark peach color. now i am in my bed and i feel drained. i am calm now. there was a strange taste of blood in the back of my throat that made me feel like i was about to get a bloody nose. today is april 19 and i am coming out of an anxiety attack.

       i wish i could live underwater
         the sea is so sweet
       she has saved me so many times
       i would let her kill me

                          i am right here
                          i am right here
                          i am right here

I'M GETTING BETTER AT
LEARNING HOW TO MEND

I HOPE YOU KNOW WHEREVER
YOU ARE I AM SENDING
YOU LOVE AND
I AM PRAYING IT BOUNCES
BACK.

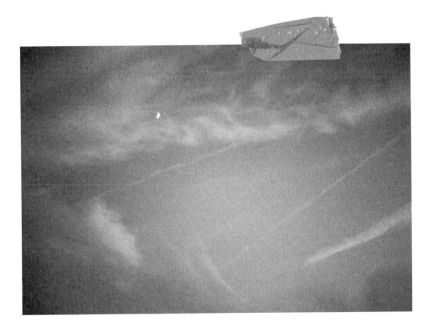

INDEX

CONTRIBUTORS

OLIVIA BEE is a photographer and director from Portland, Oregon, who is currently based in Brooklyn and Los Angeles. She is intrigued by the beauty of everyday life and how the beauty of memories (real or imagined) touches us.

TOVA BENJAMIN was born and raised in West Rogers Park, Chicago. She is currently a doctoral student in the Jewish studies department at New York University. A poet and writer, her work has appeared in *Rookie*, *Poetry*, *Nylon*, and The Hairpin, though she mostly writes letters and diary entries that occasionally appear in other people's inboxes, book anthologies, or art galleries. Her work often concerns her former Hasidic community and examines both the violence and tenderness that develop in religious interactions, as well as sexual violence and the intimate ways communities form and dissolve.

Representing five generations of the Coppola family in the film industry, **GIA COPPOLA** is not only an accomplished filmmaker, she's also a talented photographer. Born and raised in Los Angeles by her mother, Jacqui Getty, Gia graduated from Bard College in 2009 with a bachelor of fine arts degree in photography. Her artistic tendency was to use the camera with personal style, casually documenting life within her field of vision. When asked to be in a video by a friend, she declined. The friend challenged her to make her own video instead, launching her into the "behind-the-camera action" and causing her to follow in the footsteps of her grandfather, her grandmother, her aunt Sofia Coppola, and her uncle Roman Coppola. In 2014, Gia made her directorial film debut with *Palo Alto*, based on James Franco's collection of short stories.

RACHEL DAVIES is a writer living in Toronto, Canada. They've written interviews and essays for *Nylon* and *Rookie*, among many other publications. You can find them online @rachelcomplains.

SAFY HALLAN FARAH is a Somali American writer and editor. Her work has been featured in publications like *GQ*, *Vogue*, *Elle*, and *Nylon*, among others. She is currently working on a book and a few zine projects. She would love most to topple the patriarchy and get a pet poodle.

TYLER FORD is an agender writer and media personality whose creative and critical writing on queer and trans identity inspires, comforts, and challenges a diverse spectrum of audiences. Tyler's written work has appeared in many publications, including *The Guardian*, *Poetry*, *Rookie*, *V* magazine, and MTV. The twenty-seven-year-old uses their unstoppable voice, passion, and heart to uplift and advocate for queer and trans individuals worldwide.

ELEANOR HARDWICK is a photographer and director currently based in London. Her photographs and films have been exhibited in London, Paris, Tokyo, LA, Oxford, Lisbon, and Brighton, at galleries including Palais de Tokyo, the Southbank Centre, and the Cob Gallery. She has given talks at Oxford and Cambridge universities, and has been interviewed by publications such as *Dazed & Confused*, *i-D*, BBC Radio 4, British *Vogue*, *The Guardian*, The Huffington Post, *British Journal of Photography*, and *The Independent*. Hardwick's work focuses on telling political and philosophical stories of transitional and dual states, represented through the use of cameras and sound as her medium.

RUPI KAUR is a #1 *New York Times* bestselling author and illustrator of two collections of poetry. After completing her degree in rhetoric studies, she published her first collection of poems, *milk and honey*, in 2014. The internationally acclaimed collection sold well over two million copies, gracing the *New York Times* bestsellers list every week for over a year and a half. It has since been translated into over thirty languages. Her long-awaited second collection, *the sun and her flowers*, was published in 2017. Through this collection, she continues to explore a variety of themes, including love, loss, trauma, healing, femininity, migration, and revolution.

ZOÉ LAWRENCE is an artist raised between South Florida and Jamaica. Her work is a direct reflection of her upbringing. Tropical themes with the use of people of color usually find a way to shine through her photography. She began taking photos as a way to navigate around the questions she had about her own identity and eventually ventured into video work as well. She tends to deal with race and politics in her work and hopes to open dialogue about where those issues are headed.

INDIA SALVÖR MENUEZ is a genderqueer intermedia artist living and working primarily out of their hometown of NYC. They co-founded the Luck You art collective when they were fifteen, through which they first delved into curatorial work and independent publishing. The collective disbanded in 2013, after which Menuez worked in many other collaborative assemblages, most recently with 8Ball Community. Menuez's projects span contexts from the Echo Park lawn to MoMA, MoMA PS1, the New Museum, and Breakfast Club in Tokyo, to simply their own living room. With a focus on building community through collaboration, utilizing DIY as a means for accessibility, and exploring the utopian potential that is queerness, Menuez also acts, most recently starring in the Amazon show *I Love Dick*.

BELLA NEWMAN is an eighteen-year-old artist currently studying in the film discipline at NYU Tisch School of the Arts. She grew up in central Pennsylvania, where her love of photography began at age six. She is greatly infatuated with the vulnerability of individuals and the various aspects of the human condition. Bella's work has been featured in *Teen Vogue*, *Vogue*, *RUSSH*, *Oyster*, and *i-D* magazines, the book #*girlgaze: How Girls See the World*, and Playboy.com, and also has been shown at the Annenberg Space for Photography in LA, and most recently in an Adidas campaign.

GENEVIEVE NOLLINGER (b. 1999) is a photographer and filmmaker from Los Angeles, California. She began making photographs at age thirteen after receiving a camera for Christmas. Through her work, Genevieve explores how themes of intimacy, age, and autonomy exist within her life. Genevieve is currently pursuing an undergraduate education at UC Berkeley.

KARINA PADILLA is a twenty-five-year-old artist based in the Bay Area. She draws inspiration for her work from the divine feminine, using her experiences as a woman of color to create powerful imagery through personal narratives. Her work has been featured in *Artforum*, 29Rooms, and *Polyester* magazine.

SAMERA PAZ is a twenty-three-year-old artist with dreams of pursuing a career as a war photographer/photojournalist who captures the stories of people all over the world. She creates art that reflects the emotions and experiences she goes through, especially when it comes to her mental health and being a woman. She is the founder of the social organization Girl Power Meetups, and her dream is to create safe spaces for girls all over the world.

GABRIELLE RICHARDSON is a multidisciplinary artist based in NYC. Gabrielle's works range from painting, sculpture, photo, and most recently performance art. Their work mostly explores the identity and struggles of being a femme, black person in our current sociopolitical climate, an identity which at birth places you as an outlier. Gabrielle is also a curator for Art Hoe Collective, which is an online space created to give queer people of color a place to showcase their work and talent so they may receive the recognition they deserve online and off. The collective highlights the importance of identity and accessibility politics with the firm belief that if things can't be accessible then they cannot be radical.

ARABELLE SICARDI is a twenty-something beauty writer whose work focuses on the relationship between power and beauty. Their work has been in *Teen Vogue*, *Allure*, *Elle*, *i-D*, *Nylon*, *Paper*, *Rookie*, and more. They like cyborgs, perfume, and poms.

SENDRA UEBELE is a visual artist from Champaign, Illinois. She spent the last four years studying in northern Michigan and will be attending the School of the Art Institute of Chicago. Her art focuses on contemporary femininity and how that pertains to art-making and activism. She deals with ideas centered around women's work, political posters, and feminist zines.

KATI YEWELL is a twenty-year-old artist from Maryland, currently based in NYC. Kati obtained a bachelor of fine arts degree from the School of the Art Institute of Chicago under a merit scholarship. In 2016, she left school for a year and moved to NYC, where she worked as sales supervisor at Marc Jacobs's Bookmarc. Her work focuses primarily on portraiture and reworking the past into the present. With a heavy interest in literature and history, she spends a tremendous amount of her time daydreaming, writing, and dancing to jazz records. She is currently an illustrator for *Rookie* and a student at Pratt Institute.

JENNY ZHANG is a poet and writer living in New York. She is the author of the short story collection *Sour Heart* and the poetry collection *Dear Jenny, We Are All Find*.